CW01149197

Original title:
Knitted Hearts, Winter Skies

Copyright © 2024 Creative Arts Management OÜ
All rights reserved.

Author: Kieran Blackwood
ISBN HARDBACK: 978-9916-94-454-7
ISBN PAPERBACK: 978-9916-94-455-4

## **Stitched Together in the Frost**

In the stillness, whispers call,
Frosty breath as shadows fall.
Threads of silver weave the light,
Embroidered dreams in winter's night.

Hearts entwined like branches bare,
Holding warmth in chilling air.
Stitched together, we find our way,
Through frosty nights and breaking day.

**Celestial Dreams in a Winter's Night**

Stars are secrets softly spun,
Underneath the glowing sun.
In the silence, dreams take flight,
Celestial wonders in the night.

Snowflakes dance with gentle grace,
Whispers of a timeless place.
Glimmers of hope, a silver beam,
Floating softly like a dream.

## **Threads of Comfort in the Cold**

In the chill of winter's breath,
Love ignites defying death.
Woven tightly, hearts embrace,
Finding warmth in this cold space.

Hands held close through biting winds,
Together, where all warmth begins.
Threads of comfort, softly spun,
Binding two as one by one.

## The Heart's Loom in Frozen Time

Beneath a blanket of pure white,
Time stands still in frost's soft light.
The heart's loom weaves every sigh,
   Stitching moments as they fly.

Every heartbeat, a tender thread,
  Woven tales of love we've fed.
In frozen time, we find our song,
In winter's arms, where we belong.

## **Serenade of the Snowflakes' Fall**

Whispers of winter fill the air,
As snowflakes dance without a care.
They twirl and spin on velvet night,
A glimmering waltz, pure and bright.

Softly they land with gentle grace,
Each one unique, a fleeting face.
They blanket the earth in a hush,
In the stillness, hearts gently rush.

Stars peek out from a velvet sky,
As snowflakes drift and softly sigh.
Their lullabies calm the bustling night,
A serenade of pure delight.

In this magic, we find our peace,
As all worries and troubles cease.
Embraced by winter's soft embrace,
We treasure each fleeting, fragile trace.

## Radiance of Warm Touches in Chill

Fingers intertwined, a gentle hold,
In the frost's breath, warmth unfolds.
Eyes meet softly, a spark ignites,
Turning the cold into cozy nights.

A blanket wrapped, like a soft embrace,
Whispers of love in this sacred space.
With every heartbeat, embers rise,
Radiance blooms under winter skies.

## **A Cuddle Against the Winter's Bite**

As the wind howls, we nestle tight,
Wrapped in warmth, hidden from fright.
A hearth burns bright, flames dance and sway,
Together we chase the chill away.

Your breath is a balm, soothing my soul,
In your arms, I endlessly pull.
Against the winter's icy reign,
Our love shields us from all pain.

## Melodies of Comfort in the Cold

The snowflakes fall, a silent song,
In this hush, we feel we belong.
With laughter shared and stories told,
We weave sweet dreams against the cold.

Music plays softly, a soothing tune,
It cradles the night, beneath the moon.
With every note, our hearts align,
In the chill, your love is my sign.

## Love's Glow Amidst Winter's Embrace

The world is white, a canvas pure,
Yet in your gaze, I find my cure.
Your warmth surrounds me, a loving glow,
Bringing light to winter's woe.

Together we stroll through the glittering night,
Hand in hand, everything feels right.
In the frosty air, our spirits soar,
Wrapped in love, we need nothing more.

## Heartstrings in a Snowy Haven

In a quiet hush of snowfall,
Hearts entwined, we hear the call.
Softly drifting, dreams alight,
Whispers echo through the night.

Winter's canvas, pure and white,
Love ignites, a warming light.
Hand in hand, we brave the chill,
In this haven, time stands still.

## **Draped in Warmth, Wrapped in Cold**

Blankets piled, warmth like a shield,
Outside, a winter's breath revealed.
With each sip, the cocoa flows,
In our hearts, the love still grows.

Snowflakes dance on window panes,
Each a story, joy and pains.
Together we find our peace,
As the world outside will cease.

## Chasing Stars in a Wintry Twilight

Underneath a velvet sky,
We chase the stars, you and I.
Frosty air and dreams collide,
We find magic, side by side.

Whispers blend with twinkling light,
In this dance, the world feels right.
Each star shines with tales untold,
In the twilight, brave and bold.

## **Ties that Bind in Frosty Breezes**

Crisp winds carry our laughter high,
With every breath, our spirits fly.
In the frost, our shadows play,
Ties that bind, come what may.

Walking paths of shimmering white,
Hand in hand, hearts burning bright.
In this chill, our love's no pretense,
In frosty breezes, we find our sense.

## **Threads of Warmth**

In the glow of firelight's dance,
Whispers of comfort take a chance.
Soft blankets curl around each frame,
Hearts entwined in the warmest flame.

Mugs of cocoa, laughter shared,
Each moment treasured, deeply cared.
Fingers intertwined, a simple touch,
In this cocoon, we feel so much.

**Frosty Dreams**

Underneath the silver moon,
Sleepy whispers, night's sweet tune.
Snowflakes twirl in frosty air,
A dreamland woven without a care.

Blanketed in the hush of white,
Stars peek out, a gentle light.
In the cold, our dreams take flight,
Every breath a spark, a delight.

## **Stitches Beneath the Stars**

Twinkling lights in velvet skies,
Stitches woven, love never dies.
Each star a promise, bright and true,
Guiding our paths as we start anew.

Through midnight trails where shadows play,
Together we forge our own way.
In this quilt of endless night,
Hearts stitch stories, pure delight.

**Embracing the Chill**

Cold winds whisper a haunting song,
In the chill, we learn to belong.
Wrapped in layers, laughter warms,
Through frosty weather, our love transforms.

With each flake, a promise sent,
Chill and warmth, perfectly bent.
Holding close in a world so vast,
Together we brave, our love steadfast.

## **Tapestry of Love in Chill Winds**


Winds weave whispers through the trees,
Carrying tales on the brisk breeze.
Love stitched tightly, a vibrant thread,
In the tapestry where hearts are led.

Colors blend in the chilly air,
Each moment precious, bold, and rare.
Fingers entwined, we tread the night,
Creating warmth, our souls alight.

## **Silhouettes of Joy Beneath Frosty Canopies**

In the hush of morning's grace,
Shadows dance in quiet space.
Branches bow with crystal weight,
Nature whispers, love innate.

Laughter glints like fallen light,
Joyful hearts take to the flight.
Footprints trace where dreams were drawn,
In the glow of early dawn.

Every breath a chilled embrace,
Memories in winter's lace.
Frosty halos round our heads,
Warmth unfolds where love is bred.

Swaying gently, trees align,
Holding secrets, yours and mine.
Underneath the frosty sky,
Silhouettes of joy drift by.

## Lanterns of Affection in the Night

Stars above like lanterns glow,
In the night, our feelings flow.
Softly whispering sweet goodbyes,
In the darkness, love replies.

Hands entwined in shadows deep,
Promises we softly keep.
Every heartbeat, every sigh,
Guided by the moonlit sky.

Flickering hopes in candlelight,
Guiding souls through endless night.
As we wander, hearts ablaze,
In the warmth, affection stays.

Glimmers cast on faces near,
In their glow, there's nothing to fear.
Lanterns burn, a soft delight,
Keeping close our love tonight.

## **Beneath the Glint of Ice**

Beneath the glint of morning's breath,
Whispers hint of life and death.
Silent echoes fill the air,
Fragile dreams, we lay bare.

Crystals hang from branches strong,
Nature's hymn, a wintry song.
Dancing sparkles, fleeting grace,
Life reclaims its sacred space.

In the still, a kiss of sun,
Melts the barriers, one by one.
Unity through nature's eyes,
Beneath the glint, our spirits rise.

Hope awakens, winter's charm,
In the cold, there's warmth from harm.
Together here, we find our place,
Beneath the glint, love's embrace.

## Threads of Togetherness in Frost

Threads of frost in morning light,
Woven tales of pure delight.
Every sparkle holds a story,
In stillness, we find our glory.

Winter's breath, a soft caress,
Binding us in closeness, bless.
Through the chill, our warmth will weave,
Promises that we believe.

Hands in pockets, hearts laid bare,
Sharing moments with great care.
Underneath the skies of grey,
Together we will find our way.

Within the hush of drifting snow,
Strength in numbers, as we grow.
Threads connect with every frost,
In togetherness, love is embossed.

**Clouds of Comfort**

Fluffy dreams in the sky,
Drift and dance as they float by.
They wrap the world in their soft embrace,
Whispering peace in every space.

Gentle shadows in the light,
Molding day into the night.
A quiet storm of soothing grace,
Clouds of comfort we all chase.

## **Yarn of Solace**

Threads entwined with tender care,
Crafting warmth beyond compare.
In every loop, a story spun,
A tapestry of love begun.

Colors blend, a soft repose,
In every twist, a heart that knows.
Yarn of solace, woven tight,
Brings the world a gentle light.

## **Whispers of Wool Against the Cold**

In the chill, a gentle sigh,
Woolen whispers drifting high.
Soft and warm, a loving shield,
Against the frost, it never yields.

Knitted dreams in cozy night,
Huddle close, hearts feel the light.
Embraced by warmth that won't let go,
Whispers of wool against the cold.

## **Fireside Echoes in the Snow**

Crackling flames, a warm embrace,
Echoing laughter, filling space.
Outside the world, a quiet scene,
In here, the light begins to gleam.

Snowflakes dance, the night grows old,
Fireside stories, tales retold.
With every spark, a memory's glow,
Fireside echoes in the snow.

## **Patterns of Affection on Icy Nights**

Frozen stars in the sky above,
Whisper secrets of endless love.
Under blankets, we share our dreams,
In icy nights, warmth gently beams.

Each stitch, a promise carefully made,
Patterns of affection will never fade.
In the stillness, hearts knit tight,
Binding souls on quiet nights.

## Frosted Whispers Beneath the Stars

In the still of night, whispers call,
Soft as snowflakes, they rise and fall.
Under the gaze of the moon's soft light,
Frosted secrets dance in the night.

Gentle breeze carries tales untold,
Of lovers lost and dreams of old.
Footprints linger on icy ground,
Echoes of hopes that tightly wound.

Stars twinkle with a glimmering grace,
Casting shadows on time and space.
Frosted whispers seem to unite,
In the magic of this enchanting night.

As dawn breaks, the chill starts to sway,
Soft memories of night fade away.
Yet in the heart, their warmth remains,
Frosted whispers, love's sweet chains.

**Embracing Shadows in the Chill**

Cold winds weave through the barren trees,
Where shadows linger and spirits freeze.
Whispers float on the frosty air,
Embracing the night with tender care.

Moonlight spills on the icy ground,
Creating a world where dreams are found.
Figures dance in the silver sheen,
Lost in the magic, serene and keen.

Each breath is a cloud in the frigid night,
A testament to love's gentle light.
Holding close in the dark's embrace,
Finding warmth in this frozen space.

As dawn's first light begins to break,
Shadows yield to the day they awake.
Yet in our hearts, the chill remains,
Embracing love, despite the pains.

## **Celestial Tapestry of Love**

Stars collide in a cosmic dance,
Weaving tales in a timeless romance.
Threads of silver and threads of gold,
A celestial story eagerly told.

In the heart of night, dreams take flight,
Spinning softly in the moon's soft light.
Every heartbeat sings a soft tune,
Under the gaze of the watchful moon.

Galaxies spin with endless grace,
Painting a love that time can't erase.
Eternal whispers sweep through the skies,
A tapestry where love never dies.

When twilight paints the world anew,
Remember the stars and love so true.
For in the night's embrace we find,
A universe of love intertwined.

## Warmth Beneath the Icy Veil

Beneath the frost, the earth lies still,
A canvas blank, with a chilly thrill.
Yet deep within, where life entwines,
Warmth awakens, as nature designs.

Frosted edges dance in the light,
Hidden fires await the night.
Crimson embers beneath the snow,
A gentle glow, as spirits flow.

Winter whispers secrets so dear,
In the silence, love draws near.
Under the cover of icy chill,
Hearts beat fiercely, against the still.

As seasons change and thaw the cold,
Love's warm embrace shall now enfold.
Though ice may linger, truth unveils,
The warmth of love beneath icy veils.

## Hibernation of Hearts in Solitude

In winter's quiet, hearts retreat,
Beneath the snow, the pulses sleep.
Whispers of love, soft and light,
Lost in the dream of the starry night.

Time moves slow in frosty air,
Embracing silence, we find our care.
With every flake that gently falls,
A tender warmth within us calls.

Memories linger, shadows cast,
Of summer's joy, now fading fast.
Yet hope ignites a spark so bright,
In solitude, we find our light.

Through hibernation, hearts renew,
In stillness deep, we'll start anew.
For love, though wrapped in ice and snow,
Awaits the spring to softly glow.

## A Tapestry of Memories and Frost

In the chill, our stories weave,
Threads of laughter, heartaches leave.
Every layer, a moment held,
In this tapestry, we are compelled.

Frosted edges, glimmers bright,
Whispers echo in the night.
Pictures captured, forever nigh,
In the warmth of memories, we sigh.

Glistening dreams on winter's breath,
Woven tightly, a dance with death.
Yet life goes on, as hearts will beat,
In the frost, we find our seat.

So let the chill embrace us near,
For love's tapestry will persevere.
In every stitch, a promise spun,
We rise again, as one, as one.

## Radiant Love in a Winter's Embrace

In the stillness of the night,
Two hearts shine, a shared delight.
With candle glow, we find our place,
Wrapped in warmth, a gentle grace.

Snowflakes dance around our feet,
Each one unique, yet bittersweet.
In the chill, our spirits rise,
Radiant love beneath the skies.

Hand in hand, we wander far,
Guided softly by the star.
Every glance, a spark ignites,
In winter's breath, our love alights.

Through frosty panes, our dreams take flight,
In radiant love, we claim the night.
For in this embrace, time stands still,
In heartbeats' rhythm, we find our will.

## **Love Letters in Snowflakes**

Falling softly from above,
Each snowflake holds a tale of love.
Whispers carried on the breeze,
Love letters written with such ease.

Ink of winter, pure and white,
They flutter gently, pure delight.
In every swirl, a promise writes,
In fragile forms, our hearts unite.

Beneath the blanket, silence reigns,
Yet within, our passion flames.
These letters dance, so sweet and true,
In snowy realms, I think of you.

So let us gather, side by side,
In love's embrace, we shall abide.
With every flake that falls in glee,
Love letters penned for you and me.

## Gentle Murmurs Beneath the Snow

Softly falls the winter's shroud,
Whispers dance upon the ground.
Snowflakes hum a silent tune,
Blanketing the world so soon.

Branches bow with frosty grace,
Nature dons a crystal lace.
In the hush, a secret sigh,
Gentle murmurs lift on high.

Footprints trace on sparkling white,
In the stillness, hearts take flight.
Every flake a tale untold,
In the quiet, life unfolds.

Underneath the winter's glow,
Dreams awaken, softly flow.
In this world, so calm and bright,
Gentle murmurs bring delight.

## **Heartfelt Stitches of the Soul**

Threads of love weave through the night,
Binding hearts with tender light.
Every stitch a whispered prayer,
Crafting warmth from simple care.

In the fabric of our days,
Woven hopes in endless ways.
Patchwork dreams, both old and new,
Heartfelt stitches, strong and true.

Laughter echoes through each seam,
In the tapestry, we dream.
Bound together, come what may,
Hearts will find a brighter way.

With every tear, a chance to mend,
In this quilt, we'll find a friend.
Soulful threads forever twine,
In this home, our hearts align.

## Silken Threads in the Winter Wind

Glistening in the pale moonlight,
Silken threads dance, pure and bright.
Wind whispers secrets in the night,
Stitching dreams from snowy white.

Branches sway, a gentle sway,
In the cold, they find their play.
Nature's breath, a soft embrace,
Silken threads in winter's grace.

Stars twinkle in the velvet sky,
As frosty breezes waltz nearby.
Every gust a story spun,
In the chill, we feel the fun.

Together, we shall weave our tale,
In the wintry night, we'll sail.
Silken threads of joy unroll,
Binding us, a shared soul.

## Kindred Spirits Beneath Frozen Heavens

Beneath the stars, a bond so rare,
Kindred spirits, hearts laid bare.
Frozen heavens watch with grace,
Together, we have found our place.

In the stillness, laughter rings,
Frigid air, yet warmth it brings.
Hand in hand, we dare to tread,
Paths of light where angels led.

Every moment, pure delight,
In the dark, we shine so bright.
Underneath the icy sky,
Kindred souls will always fly.

When the world is cold and gray,
Together, we'll find our way.
In this journey, side by side,
Kindred spirits, love our guide.

## **Beneath a Blanket of Snow**

Softly falls the winter's quilt,
A hush across the silent field.
Blanket white on earth is built,
Nature sleeps, her fate revealed.

Frozen breath in twilight glows,
Footprints trace a path in white.
Trees wear crowns of sparkling prose,
Underneath the stars so bright.

## **Whispers of Love in a Polar Embrace**

In the chill of evening's light,
Two hearts warm the frozen night.
With each whisper soft and near,
Love's sweet echo, crystal clear.

Hands entwined, like vines they grow,
The world narrows, just they know.
In the dance of snowflakes' flight,
Passion melts the frosty bite.

## Echoes of Warmth in the Frosty Air

By the flames, the shadows play,
Stories fold and weave their sway.
Echoes of laughter fill the space,
In this warmth, we find our place.

Frosted windows hide the night,
Yet inside glows a soft light.
Lift your cup and toast the cheer,
Every heartbeat sharp and clear.

## **Interlaced Dreams Beneath the Snow**

Dreams are spun in frosty threads,
Beneath the cloak where silence treads.
Imagination's snowy flight,
Whispers dance in the pale light.

Layers deep, our hopes shall rest,
Cradled here, the heart's own nest.
When spring calls and all awakes,
New dreams bloom, the earth remakes.

## Beneath the Layered Skies

Clouds drift softly in the blue,
Painting dreams we wish were true.
Whispers of the winds so mild,
Nature's secrets, sweet and wild.

Sunset tinges the horizon bright,
Casting shadows, warming night.
Beneath the layered skies we lay,
Embracing dusk, forgetting day.

## **Emblems of Togetherness in the Frost**

Frosty breath hangs in the air,
In every glance, a tender stare.
Snowflakes dance like whispered words,
Emblems of love that swiftly blurs.

Hand in hand, we leave our trace,
In winter's chill, we find our place.
Beneath the stars, we carve our fate,
Together always, never late.

## Cozy Embrace Under a Celestial Canvas

In a nook by the firelight,
We share our dreams, silent and bright.
Stars above begin to glow,
Guiding us to where love flows.

Wrapped in warmth, our spirits soar,
Every heartbeat, we love more.
Under a celestial canvas wide,
In this moment, we abide.

## **Crafting Affection Amidst Winter's Gaze**

Winter's breath chills the night air,
Yet here with you, there's warmth to share.
Crafting affection with each soft touch,
In the cold, we find our clutch.

Glistening ice paints the world bright,
In your eyes, I see such light.
With every moment, love we seize,
Amidst winter's gaze, hearts at ease.

## The Warmth of Togetherness in a Winter's Tale

In the hush of falling snow,
We gather close, our laughter low.
Blankets wrapped, a fire's glow,
Hearts aglow as cold winds blow.

Each whispered secret, soft and sweet,
Fingers entwined, a gentle beat.
Outside, the world is dressed in white,
Inside, we bask in love's warm light.

Through frosted glass, we watch the scene,
Winter's wonder, a holiday dream.
Sipping cocoa, a shared delight,
Together we shine on this starry night.

As time slows down, the night unfolds,
Moments cherished, stories told.
In this winter's tale, we find our place,
In the warmth of love's embrace.

## **Memories Woven in White**

Snowflakes dance on the chilly breeze,
Each one falls with exquisite ease.
Moments captured, the world so bright,
Memories woven in purest white.

Footprints trace where we used to roam,
In winter's hush, we build our home.
Laughter echoes in the crisp air,
Every glance tells how much we care.

The warmth of voices in the night,
In silence share our pure delight.
Hot chocolate swirls, marshmallows float,
Together, our dreams gently coat.

Through the window, a blanket of snow,
Nestled in dreams, we let love grow.
Memories linger, sweet and grand,
In the winter's chill, we forever stand.

## A Winter's Caress: Tender Moments

With each touch, the cold retreats,
A winter's caress, soft and sweet.
Holding hands as daylight fades,
In tender moments, love cascades.

Under stars that brightly twinkle,
Hearts aligned, our souls do sprinkle.
The night whispers, secrets shared,
In this calm, we are ensnared.

Snow blankets all, a peaceful sight,
We weave our stories in candlelight.
Every heartbeat, a promise made,
In winter's arms, our fears allayed.

Through frosty breath, we sing a tune,
Rich with warmth like a balmy June.
Together we dance in the evening air,
As winter's magic ignites our care.

## **Frosted Poetry in the Air**

Whispers of frost weave tales anew,
In every flake, a poem true.
The world adorned in a crystal hue,
Frosted poetry, a winter view.

With every step, a crunching sound,
Nature's rhythm, all around.
The chill is sharp, yet hearts are warm,
In this season, love takes form.

Carols echo through the night,
Chasing shadows with pure delight.
Beneath the stars, our breath like mist,
In winter's spell, we find our bliss.

So let us gather, hand in hand,
Embrace the magic, understand.
In every moment, love laid bare,
There's frosted poetry in the air.

## **Hearthside Verses of Warmth**

In the glow of amber light,
We gather close, hearts ignite.
Whispers dance upon the air,
Comfort found in warmth we share.

Crackling flames, a soothing song,
As shadows flicker, night grows long.
Stories told with laughter's grace,
Creating memories in this place.

The world outside is cold and bleak,
Yet here we find the warmth we seek.
Mugs of cocoa, scents of pine,
In this moment, all is fine.

So let the winter winds howl and sway,
In our hearthside haven, we'll laugh and play.
Wrapped in warmth, our spirits gleam,
Together, we'll weave a radiant dream.

## **Dreaming in a Soft Embrace**

Under blankets, dreams take flight,
Whispers float into the night.
Gentle breezes through the trees,
Comforted by silken ease.

Stars above like distant light,
Guide our hearts through velvet night.
In this world, so soft, so sweet,
With every heartbeat, love's heartbeat.

Images of joy cascade,
In this sanctuary we've made.
Fingers intertwined so tight,
In a realm of love, pure and bright.

Tomorrow's worries fade away,
As we linger, here we'll stay.
Drifting in a soft embrace,
In our hearts, a timeless space.

## Threads of Memory in Swirling Snow

Snowflakes fall, a silent dance,
Each one holds a fleeting chance.
To recall the days of yore,
Moments cherished, hearts adore.

Footprints fade as new ones form,
Yet memories uniquely warm.
Laughter echoes through the years,
Crafting joy from joy and tears.

Around the fires, tales unfold,
Of adventures brave and bold.
In swirling snow, we lose our way,
But memories guide us on display.

Threads of time, woven tight,
Crafting dreams from day to night.
In winter's grip, we find our flow,
Creating warmth in swirling snow.

## Gathering Warmth in Frigid Air

In the chill of evening's breath,
We gather close, defying death.
Hearts ablaze with every word,
In this space, peace is stirred.

Frosted windows, twilight gleams,
We share the weight of whispered dreams.
Layers thick, but spirits light,
In each other, futures bright.

The world is cold, but we are bold,
Stories shared and tales retold.
Unity in the frosty night,
With every laugh, our hearts take flight.

So let the frosty winds arise,
We'll raise our voices to the skies.
In this gathering, warmth we find,
In frigid air, our souls entwined.

## **Twisted Fibers and Snowflakes' Dance**

In the quiet night, snowflakes twirl,
Each one unique, a gentle pearl.
Fibers weave tales of warmth and glow,
As winter's breath begins to blow.

Through branches bare and skies of gray,
The dance of snow takes breath away.
Twisted fibers bind us tight,
Under soft blankets of pure white.

Whispers of stories, soft and sweet,
In the tapestry of life, we meet.
Together we spin in nature's trance,
Lost in the magic of winter's dance.

As dawn breaks through the frosted trees,
The world is hushed, a perfect freeze.
With every snowflake, a dream unfurls,
In twisted fibers and snowflakes' swirls.

## **The Fabric of Solitude**

In solitude's embrace, I find my way,
Threads of silence where shadows play.
Each stitch a memory, worn yet bright,
A tapestry woven in the soft night.

The fabric whispers of dreams long past,
Moments captured, shadows cast.
In the stillness, echoes softly hum,
A lullaby of the heart's quiet drum.

Colors fade into the twilight's sigh,
With every heartbeat, time drifts by.
Wrapped in solitude, I learn to see,
The beauty that blooms in the absence of thee.

As the stars emerge in the inky deep,
The fabric of solitude cradles my sleep.
A cloak of peace, a gentle balm,
In the heart's quiet chamber, I find my calm.

## Heartbeats in a Blanket of White

Underneath the snow, the earth lies still,
Each heartbeat muffled by winter's chill.
A blanket of white, soft and round,
Hides the secrets buried in the ground.

The world transformed, a canvas pure,
Where heartbeats echo, faint but sure.
Every flake that falls, a sweet embrace,
In this tranquil space, we find our place.

Glistening crystals in the pale moonlight,
Mirroring dreams that twinkle bright.
Heartbeats synchronize with the frost,
In the blanket of white, never lost.

As dawn greets softly with a golden hue,
Life stirs beneath, fresh and new.
In each gentle whisper, we feel the grace,
Heartbeats in a blanket, time we trace.

## **Echoes of Togetherness Through Flurries**

In the heart of winter, flurries fall,
Whispers of warmth in the frostbitten call.
Each flake a moment, a shared embrace,
Echoes of laughter in the quiet space.

Together we wander through drifts of white,
Hands held tight in the fading light.
Footsteps crunch on the snow-laden ground,
As echoes of joy in the air abound.

The world is hushed, but our spirits soar,
In every flurry, we find the core.
Together we dance, lost in the flares,
In echoes of love, our heart declares.

As twilight descends with a gentle sigh,
Our togetherness glimmers in the sky.
Through flurries we journey, hearts intertwined,
In the echo of winter, our souls aligned.

## **Serenity Found in Frosty Embraces**

Snowflakes dance in twilight's glow,
Whispers of peace in silence flow.
Blankets white on a slumbering ground,
In frosty arms, true calm is found.

Moonlit nights cast a silver hue,
Stars in the sky, like dreams come true.
Nature wraps in a frozen hug,
Cradled softly, a subtle drug.

Each breath is crisp, a breath of air,
Frosty kisses are quiet, rare.
In winter's grasp, we find our rest,
Tranquility feels so blessed.

With every flake that softly lands,
Serenity is where the heart stands.
Where icy whispers tell their tale,
In winter's charm, we gently sail.

## **The Ties of Affection in Chill**

Fingers entwined, warmth in the cold,
Stories of love quietly told.
Under the sky painted in frost,
In each other's arms, nothing is lost.

Laughter echoes through the snowy trees,
Wrapped together, we catch the breeze.
Hearts like fire on a winter day,
Ignite the chill, chase gloom away.

Softly we wander, dressed in white,
Chasing shadows, embracing the night.
In the hush where the wild winds play,
Our affection glows, bright as the day.

Frozen moments, forever we claim,
Through chilly paths, we're never the same.
Building a bond, like snowflakes true,
In this wonderland, just me and you.

# **Refuge in a White Wonderland**

In a world sheathed in glistening white,
We found our haven, pure delight.
Each tree a castle, each hill a dream,
In winter's embrace, we flow like a stream.

Gentle whispers of the falling snow,
A sanctuary where hearts can grow.
Footprints trace where our love once ran,
In the white wonder, united we stand.

The air is crisp, a refreshing drink,
In frozen stillness, we pause and think.
Wrapped in nature's precious spell,
In this quiet place, all is well.

Through frosty nights, with stars in view,
Our bond grows stronger, forever true.
In snowy landscapes, we find our way,
Together in this wonderland, we stay.

## **Hearts Bound by Icy Twists**

Tangled thoughts in the winter's chill,
Ice and warmth weave through will.
Hearts entwined by frost's fine lace,
In icy twists, we find our place.

Through swirling winds, our laughter flies,
A melody beneath gray skies.
Each moment stirs, like snowflakes bright,
In the depths of winter, love takes flight.

Watches the world through crystal eyes,
A frozen prism, where beauty lies.
Together we dance, in rhythms slow,
With every heartbeat, our spirits glow.

In the embrace of this stunning frost,
We count our blessings, cherish the lost.
Bound by the chilly breath of fate,
In icy twists, our hearts elate.

## Heartfelt Whispers in Frozen Breezes

In the hush of winter's breath,
Soft whispers echo near.
Frosted flakes dance gently down,
Each flake a fleeting tear.

Underneath the silver moon,
Promises linger still.
Embers of warmth within our hearts,
Time frozen, yet we feel.

Beneath the stars, our secrets shared,
In shadows softly cast.
With each gentle wind that blows,
These memories hold fast.

In this realm of whispered dreams,
Together we still roam.
Heartfelt tales in frigid air,
This frozen world our home.

## **Starlit Serenity on Chilled Nights**

Beneath the endless, gleaming sky,
Stars weave a calming lace.
Whispers of the night unfold,
In silver's warm embrace.

Snowflakes glisten on the ground,
Each one a song untold.
In quiet moments shared with you,
Our love begins to unfold.

Echoes of laughter fill the air,
As twilight starts to fade.
In the chill of starlight's grip,
Together, unafraid.

A serenade of dreams portrayed,
In shadows softly spun.
Wrapped in your serene presence,
The night is never done.

## **Interwoven Remembrances of Love**

In every thread of time we weave,
A tapestry unfolds.
Whispers of the heart emerge,
As stories long retold.

Fingers graze the fabric fine,
Each moment we embrace.
In the quiet, love ignites,
A journey we retrace.

Across the years, through seasons bright,
The threads of us entwine.
With every stitch, a promise made,
Together, hearts align.

Memories like colors blend,
In patterns bold and sweet.
In the loom of life we find,
Love's tapestry complete.

# **Eternal Flame in a Snowy World**

In the stillness of the night,
A spark against the frost.
An eternal flame ignites,
In the cold, never lost.

Through swirling snow, we journey on,
Hand in hand, hearts aglow.
The warmth of love, a guiding light,
In a world draped in snow.

Every flake, a gentle kiss,
A promise to hold dear.
In this winter's wonderland,
Our path is clear, no fear.

With every step, our hearts expand,
An inferno beneath the chill.
In this snowy realm of dreams,
Eternally, love will.

## Shadows Dancing Beneath Starry Canopies

In the hush of night, shadows sway,
Beneath the stars that softly play.
Whispers of dreams drift in the air,
As moonlight dances, bright and fair.

Flickering lights in the silent sky,
Echoes of wishes that linger nigh.
Each twinkle holds a story untold,
Of love and courage, brave and bold.

Silhouettes twirl in a magical trance,
Lost in the rhythm of twilight's dance.
Nature's embrace, a gentle delight,
Cradling secrets on this starry night.

As dawn approaches, the shadows flee,
Yet in our hearts, they'll always be.
Reminders of moments, fleeting and bright,
Shadows that linger beyond the light.

## Serene Embrace in Winter's Touch

A blanket of white drapes the land,
Nature sleeps under winter's hand.
In the stillness, peace resides,
Among the trees where silence hides.

Frosty breath of the morning air,
Whispers of warmth, a gentle prayer.
With every flake that softly falls,
The world transforms, as magic calls.

Footsteps crunch on the frozen ground,
In this serene space, solace is found.
Hot cocoa steaming, lips held warm,
Within this hush, hearts are reborn.

Through the chill, love's light remains,
Binding us close through icy chains.
Together we find joy and mirth,
In winter's touch, a new rebirth.

**Frost-kissed Dreams and Quiet Moments**

In the quiet dawn, dreams arise,
Frost-kissed whispers greet the skies.
Morning dew, a jeweled lace,
Nature's breath in a tranquil space.

Softly drifting, thoughts take flight,
Wrapped in warmth, away from plight.
Each fleeting moment, a treasure found,
Echoes of peace in a world unbound.

Candles flicker in the deepening hush,
Mornings adorned with a gentle blush.
With every sip of the herbal brew,
Quiet moments become fresh anew.

As sunlight bathes the sleeping trees,
Frost-kissed dreams float with ease.
In this embrace, time takes its rest,
A sanctuary where hearts are blessed.

## Resilience Wrapped in Soft Yarns

From tangled threads, stories are spun,
Resilience woven, one by one.
Colors of courage, vibrant and bright,
Stitch by stitch, they bring forth light.

In moments of sorrow, we bind and weave,
Creating a tapestry we won't grieve.
Softness encases the battles fought,
With each loop, a lesson taught.

Yarns of connection, each tightly knit,
Fostering strength where shadows sit.
In the patterns, echoes of hope,
A guiding thread, helping us cope.

Wrapped in warmth, we stand as one,
From fragile fibers, we've all begun.
Resilience flows through every seam,
In the fabric of life, we chase our dream.

**Embraced by the Elemental**

Whispers of wind through ancient trees,
The soft murmur of the flowing seas,
Embers dance in twilight's embrace,
Nature's rhythm, a sacred space.

Mountains rise with a silent call,
Cascading rivers, they never fall,
Clouds weave stories in the bright sky,
With every breath, the earth's sweet sigh.

Fires crackle in the dark of night,
Stars twinkle, a magical sight,
In every corner, life's embrace,
Elemental peace, a warm grace.

## Seasons of Bonding Beneath Glistening Veils

Spring whispers secrets in soft blooms,
Summer dances in bright marigloom,
Autumn paints leaves in rust and gold,
Winter wraps all in tales retold.

Each season a tapestry of grace,
In nature's arms, we find our place,
Together we gather, hearts entwined,
Beneath glistening veils, love defined.

Moments shared in sun and rain,
Through laughter, joy, and even pain,
A bond unbroken, forever true,
Seasons change, but love renews.

## The Gentle Touch of Yarns and Stars

Threads of silver, woven with care,
Stars above seem to glimmer and stare,
Yarns of laughter, colors of dreams,
In our hearts, the soft glow beams.

Knitting moments, one stitch at a time,
Embroidered stories, a rhythm sublime,
With every pattern, a memory made,
In the tapestry of love, never to fade.

Gentle whispers in twilight's glow,
Crafting connections, tender and slow,
Fabric of life, both sturdy and light,
Together we weave, hearts shining bright.

## **Harmony in Every Loop and Stitch**

In every loop, a story begins,
A dance of yarn where friendship wins,
Stitches in time, a rhythmic embrace,
Crafting together in this sacred space.

Harmony flows in colors that blend,
With every thread, we mend and intend,
A world united, in love we trust,
In the fabric of life, we weave the just.

Hands intertwined, hearts open wide,
Through every row, we take in stride,
A masterpiece born from care and thought,
In the gentle art, we find what we sought.

## Luminescent Hearts in the Gloom

In shadows deep, where silence lies,
Two hearts beat soft, beneath the skies.
A warmth ignites, a gentle spark,
Together strong, they brave the dark.

With whispered dreams, they share their fears,
Through tangled nights, and hidden tears.
A guiding light, a love so bright,
Illuminates the longest night.

Their laughter dances on the breeze,
A melody that brings them ease.
In gloom they find a glowing hue,
Two souls as one, forever true.

## **Frigid Nights and Loving Light**

In winter's grasp, the cold winds bite,
Yet hearts unite, igniting light.
Through frosted panes, the stars align,
A beacon shines, two souls entwine.

Beneath the moon, their whispers blend,
In secret vows, love will not end.
A fire ignites, defying chill,
With every breath, they warm the thrill.

As snowflakes fall, they dance in time,
A waltz of warmth, a rhythm prime.
Through frigid nights, their love takes flight,
A gentle glow, a pure delight.

## Embers of Affection in the Cold

Amidst the frost, their embers glimmer,
With every touch, the warmth grows thicker.
In icy trails, their laughter swells,
A love that sings, a story tells.

With every breath, their passions flare,
In tender moments, hearts laid bare.
Through winter's chill, a fire inside,
Together strong, they will abide.

As blankets wrap, they dream of spring,
But in the cold, their hearts take wing.
Embers dance, igniting the night,
With love as their true guiding light.

## Twinkling Lights in a Silvery Shroud

Beneath the stars, in silver sheen,
They watch the world, serene, unseen.
With twinkling lights that softly glow,
Their love ignites, a gentle flow.

Through whispered words, their hopes take flight,
In every glance, ignites the night.
The universe, a canvas wide,
With dreams and wishes cast inside.

As twilight fades, the night expands,
Together close, with entwined hands.
In silvery shrouds, they find their way,
With twinkling lights that softly play.

## Emblazoned Memories in Wintry Dreams

Snowflakes dance in swirling hues,
Whispers of warmth in the night's embrace.
Each memory wrapped in frosty blues,
As stars ignite the tranquil space.

Silent paths stretch far and wide,
Footprints tracing stories long.
In this hush, our hearts abide,
While winter sings its timeless song.

Candles flicker, shadows play,
Fireside tales of joy and cheer.
Through icy realms where dreams stray,
The hearth's glow draws us near.

Glimmers of laughter, bittersweet,
With every breath, a tale unfolds.
In the quiet, our spirits meet,
Emblazoned memories, treasures bold.

## **Frostbitten Embraces and Warm Souls**

Frosty air bites at tender cheeks,
Yet warmth ignites in hearts so bright.
Amidst the chill, love gently speaks,
A cozy glow against the night.

Wrapped in blankets, whispers sweet,
We share our hopes beside the fire.
Each heart's rhythm, a steady beat,
Fueling dreams, stoking desire.

Outside the window, snowflakes fall,
A silvery quilt on earth's sweet bed.
With every flake, the world stands tall,
While warmth surrounds what's softly said.

We cherish moments, pure, sincere,
In frostbitten embraces, love swells.
Through winter's grasp, we hold what's dear,
Warm souls amidst the icy spells.

## The Knapsack of Winter's Dreams

In a knapsack, memories reside,
Nestled tight, a treasure trove.
Wrapped in snowflakes, side by side,
Winter's essence, a tale to strove.

Each heartbeat echoes through the frost,
Like whispers of joy in twilight's glow.
Nothing precious, nothing lost,
Just dreams carried where shadows flow.

With every chill, a wish is spun,
Across the fields of white they glide.
Under the watchful, gleaming sun,
Our hopes blossom, our hearts abide.

Take this knapsack, venture wide,
Across the mists, through frozen streams.
In winter's grace, let love be our guide,
Wandering souls, full of dreams.

# **Beneath the Echo of Winter's Heart**

Beneath the echo, silence reigns,
Soft whispers drift on icy air.
Time pauses, while magic remains,
In winter's heart, all burdens bare.

Stars sparkle like diamonds, so bright,
Casting shadows on glistening snow.
Each moment, a glimpse of pure light,
As the moon smiles, soft and slow.

Through tranquil nights, our spirits soar,
Wrapped in dreams of frost and fire.
In the embrace, we seek for more,
Where winter's tale lifts hearts higher.

So let us wander, lost and found,
In the echoes of winter's art.
As memories twirl all around,
Beneath the echo of winter's heart.

## **A Shelter from the Frost**

In the hush of winter's breath,
A haven waits from cold and death.
With walls of warmth and love spread wide,
Inside, the heart will not abide.

Cocoa steam rises in the air,
Laughter dances, light and rare.
The world outside is harsh and gray,
But here, our joys will always stay.

Fire crackles with tales untold,
Embers flicker, bright and bold.
Together, we will face the freeze,
For warmth is found in moments seized.

## Love Weaved in Twilight

Beneath the sky, a canvas glows,
With gentle hues, as summer slows.
In whispered words and eyes that shine,
Our hearts create a love divine.

The stars emerge, a soft embrace,
With every glance, we find our place.
Twilight's magic in the air,
In tender smiles, we weave our care.

Fingers touch as shadows blend,
In this sweet moment, hearts will mend.
Together, we shall chase the night,
For love is found in soft twilight.

## Chilly Breezes, Warm Connections

Chilly breezes through the trees,
Carry laughter on the breeze.
Hats pulled low, we shuffle close,
In the warmth of love, we boast.

Scarves wrapped tight, a bond we share,
With every breath, a laugh in the air.
In winter's chill, we find our heat,
Every heartbeat feels so sweet.

As the frost lays its gentle kiss,
We find the warmth in moments missed.
Chilly winds may swirl and race,
Yet in your arms, I find my place.

## Underneath the Twinkling Silence

Underneath the stars' soft glow,
In whispered dreams, our feelings flow.
Silence speaks in tender sighs,
As constellations light the skies.

Moonlight bathes the world in grace,
In your gaze, I find my place.
With every twinkle overhead,
Our hearts in silence, gently tread.

Embracing hues of night and day,
In twilight's cloak, we drift and sway.
The universe, our witness bright,
In warm connections, hearts take flight.

## Melting Hearts in the Coldest Hours

In winter's clutch, we stand so near,
Your whispered warmth, it draws me here.
With icy breath, the night is bold,
Yet love's soft fire begins to unfold.

As frostbite kisses our gloved hands,
We weave a tale of heart's commands.
Beneath the chill, our laughter rings,
Two melting hearts, the season brings.

A snowflake's dance, a fleeting chance,
In silent dreams, we share a glance.
With every breath, the cold retreats,
In tender warmth, our spirit meets.

Embracing hope in wintry days,
We'll find the light in endless ways.
Through frozen nights, our love will soar,
Two melting hearts, forevermore.

## **Candlelight Among Frosted Pines**

Beneath the trees where shadows lay,
The candles flicker, chase night away.
Frosted pines stand tall and grand,
Together we've made this whispered stand.

A glow that warms the frozen air,
In every light, a secret share.
Through every flicker, stories told,
Of warmth we seek and love so bold.

In twilight's grasp, we find our way,
Each candle's glow, a promise made.
Among the pines, hope softly shines,
In winter's heart, our love entwines.

The night grows deep, the world asleep,
Yet in this glow, our dreams we keep.
Together here, in shadow's dance,
With candlelight, we take our chance.

## **Breath of Love Against the Frost**

The air is crisp, but hearts are warm,
Your touch a shield against the storm.
In every sigh, a breath of love,
Together we rise, like stars above.

Frosty whispers curl in the night,
Yet deep within, our spirits light.
Each step we take, the world refrains,
In love's embrace, the cold contains.

With every heartbeat, we withstand,
This frozen world, we understand.
Through icy veins, our pulses race,
In breath of love, we find our place.

The chill may bite, the wind may howl,
But in your eyes, there's no more scowl.
The frost may linger, yet we stand,
Against it all, united and planned.

## **Unity Under Glistening Stars**

In the canopy of night, we lie,
Glistening stars in velvet sky.
With gentle hands, we reach as one,
Under the watchful moon, we run.

Each twinkle speaks of dreams we've shared,
In every moment, love declared.
Together, bound by cosmic ties,
Our unity beneath the skies.

The world drifts on, but we remain,
In starlit whispers, hopes sustain.
Through darkest nights, we find our way,
Guided by light, come what may.

Embracing all that life may bring,
With every heartbeat, sweetly sing.
Under the stars, our truth shines bright,
Together we dance, in love's pure light.

## Layers of Comfort Against the Dark

In the quiet night, shadows play,
Soft whispers weave through dreams astray.
Blankets wrap around the weary heart,
A cocoon where all the fears depart.

Flickering flames in the hearth glow bright,
Casting warmth against the lonely night.
Each flicker tells of tales untold,
Of courage found, and hearts that bold.

Within these walls, laughter echoes clear,
A shelter built, where love draws near.
Every corner holds a cherished grace,
Familiar smiles, a warm embrace.

As dawn approaches, shadows fade away,
Layers of comfort greet the day.
With open arms, we rise to meet,
The world anew, with joy, complete.

## **Embracing the Cold**

The chill in the air bites like a knife,
Yet within the frost, there is new life.
Snowflakes dance in their graceful flight,
Each one a gem in the pale moonlight.

Bundle me warmly in layers tight,
As we wander through the winter night.
Breath becomes clouds in the crisp, clear sky,
In this frozen world, we live and sigh.

Hands held close against the cutting breeze,
Together we find warmth, hearts at ease.
With every step, the world feels right,
Embracing the cold, our spirits ignite.

Through cracked branches, the stars brightly shine,
Guiding our path, your hand in mine.
The cold may bite, but we stand tall,
In each other's warmth, we will never fall.

## Singing Together

Voices rise like the morning sun,
In harmony, our hearts become one.
Melodies weave through the open air,
A chorus of love, free from despair.

In laughter's glimmer and fragile breeze,
We sing our dreams, our hopes with ease.
Each note holds the stories we share,
Binding our souls in this moment rare.

With every verse, the world falls away,
In the magic of song, forever we stay.
A melody sweet, where spirits soar,
Together we sing, forevermore.

Through valleys deep and mountains high,
In every whisper and joyful sigh.
We find our strength in the songs we sing,
United as one, in this beautiful spring.

## **Love Stitched into the Fabric of Time**

Every stitch tells tales of old,
Of love woven deep, a thread of gold.
In twilight's glow, we find our way,
Together we dance, come what may.

As seasons change and years drift by,
Our love remains, a soft, sweet sigh.
Through tangled paths and winding roads,
Together we carry each other's loads.

In every moment, fragments align,
Crafting a tapestry, truly divine.
The fabric of time, both fragile and strong,
Threads of our lives in a timeless song.

With each heartbeat, the pattern unfolds,
Stories entwined, our past retold.
Love stitched securely, forever will shine,
A masterpiece crafted, your hand in mine.

## **Woven Threads of Solitude**

In silence deep, where shadows creep,
Woven threads of solitude we keep.
Among the thoughts that softly flow,
A tapestry of dreams begins to grow.

The stillness wraps around like night,
In quiet corners, a hidden light.
Reflections glimmer in the mind's wide sea,
Woven threads whisper, 'Just be free.'

Echoes of time drift gently past,
In moments held, the world stands fast.
Each breath a stitch, each pulse a rhyme,
In woven solitude, we find our time.

As stars above paint stories bright,
In woven threads, we find our light.
Each strand a promise, a memory's grace,
In solitude's bosom, we find our place.

Milton Keynes UK
Ingram Content Group UK Ltd.
UKHW021240191124
451300UK00007B/165